PRACTISE TOGETHER SERIES

CALCULATOR SKILLS 2

Alan Brighouse
David Godber
Peter Patilla

A Piccolo Original
Piccolo Books

A note to parents

Calculator Skills 1 and 2 are designed for children between the ages of 7 – 11. The age ranges on the books are, of course, approximate and should not be taken as a rigid guideline as children's mathematical skills develop at very different rates.

These books have been designed to complement and reinforce much of the mathematics taught at school, but they use a more informal approach. The calculator activities have been selected to increase and enrich the child's mathematical ability, as well as to give confidence in using a calculator. The main aims of the books are to:

develop mathematical thinking
explore number patterns
encourage and improve the ability to estimate
reinforce known concepts
develop new concepts

Calculators allow these areas to be developed.

Calculator Skills encourages children to work at their own pace. Occasionally they may call for help. When this happens, don't give your child the answer. Rather, attempt by your questions to encourage the child to find the solution for herself. Give plenty of praise. The pages of the book can be done in any order. Some pages may be slightly more difficult than others so do not let the child become bogged down in an activity.

It is important that the work is taken in small stages. The activities are there to be enjoyed. When they stop being fun, it is time for a rest and a change. Therefore encourage the child to work in short bursts. Don't keep her at it until it becomes a chore.

There are parent notes on some of the pages which give useful advice on the nature of the activities on the page. These are there as a guide only if you wish to work more closely with the child.
(*In order to avoid using he/she,/him/her,* we have referred to the child as 'she' in these notes.)

Your involvement and interest is of the greatest importance, and although the activities can be tackled by the child alone, we hope the books will provide opportunities for discussion between you.

1 TABLE TEASER

A square and a rectangle have been drawn on the table square.
Multiply the numbers in the opposite corners together.

The square:

4 × 16 = ☐   8 × 8 = ☐

The rectangle:

18 × 42 = ☐   21 × 36 = ☐

1	2	3	4	5	6	7	8	9	10	11	12
2	4	6	8	10	12	14	16	18	20	22	24
3	6	9	12	15	18	21	24	27	30	33	36
4	8	12	16	20	24	28	32	36	40	44	48
5	10	15	20	25	30	35	40	45	50	55	60
6	12	18	24	30	36	42	48	54	60	66	72
7	14	21	28	35	42	49	56	63	70	77	84
8	16	24	32	40	48	56	64	72	80	88	96
9	18	27	36	45	54	63	72	81	90	99	108
10	20	30	40	50	60	70	80	90	100	110	120
11	22	33	44	55	66	77	88	99	110	121	132
12	24	36	48	60	72	84	96	108	120	132	144

What do you notice?
Draw some more squares and rectangles on the table square.
Multiply the corner numbers.
What do you notice?

The child should notice that by multiplying opposite corners the result is the same. Identical results will be found regardless of size or shape of the rectangle or square. This activity develops a child's understanding of the structure of number, eg 6 × 6 is the same as 3 × 12.

2 CONQUER THE MOON

Use each rocket once.
Add its number to any number on the launch pad.
If the total is on the moon, cover it with a counter (or a coin).
If you cover all the numbers you have conquered the moon.

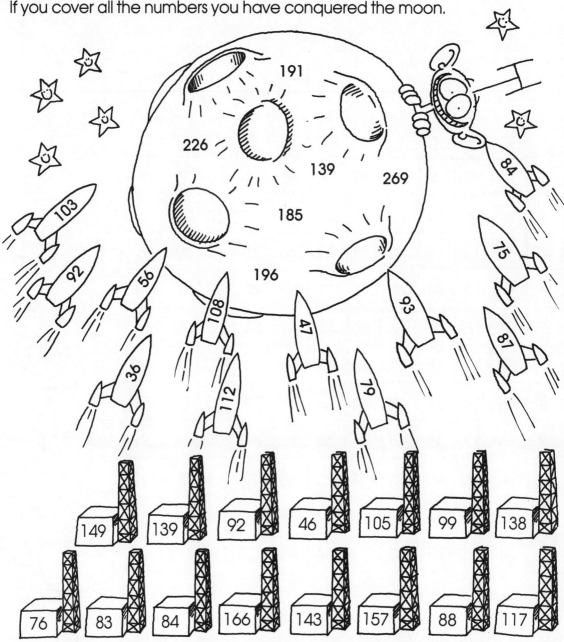

If you run out of rockets, take all the counters off and start again.

To launch the rockets successfully the child should be encouraged to look at the answers on the moon first and then find suitable number pairs.

3 SPECIAL KEYS

Try to make the number using only the keys shown.
Use the boxes to show how you did it.
The first one is done for you.

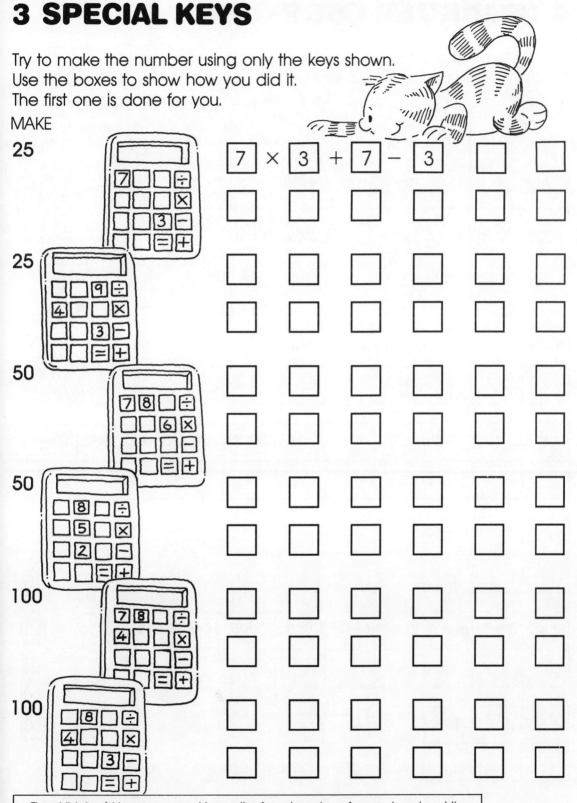

MAKE

25    $7 \times 3 + 7 - 3$

25

50

50

100

100

The child should be encouraged to use the fewest number of moves to arrive at the
answer, eg 7 × 3 as an opening move is quicker than 7 + 7 + 7.

4 CRACK THE CODE

Find the meaning of the coded message.
Use the circular codes to help you.

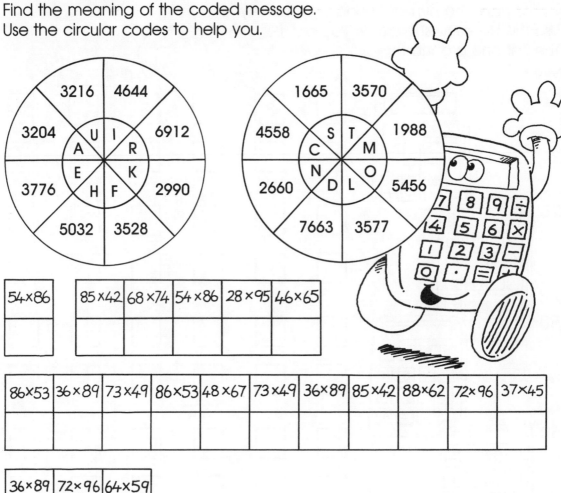

54×86

85×42	68×74	54×86	28×95	46×65

86×53	36×89	73×49	86×53	48×67	73×49	36×89	85×42	88×62	72×96	37×45

36×89	72×96	64×59

85×42	72×96	64×59	71×28	64×59	28×95	79×97	88×62	48×67	37×45

49×72	48×67	28×95

Accurate use of the calculator is essential in order to achieve the correct answers. The child should be encouraged to look for repeated examples to save time.

5 TURN AND TURN AGAIN

Write any three digit number.
The first digit must be at
least 2 bigger than the last.

Reverse the number.

Subtract the numbers.

Reverse the answer.

Add the last two rows of numbers.

Try with some three digit numbers of your own:

Write any three digit number.
The first digit must be at
least 2 bigger than the last.

Reverse the number.

Subtract the numbers.

Reverse the answer.

Add the last two rows of numbers.

Write any three digit number.
The first digit must be at
least 2 bigger than the last.

Reverse the number.

Subtract the numbers.

Reverse the answer.

Add the last two rows of numbers.

What do you notice?

The calculator is a useful tool for exploring number patterns. The child may want to try again with other numbers.

6 PYRAMID PATTERNS

Use your calculator for the first three examples.
Try and guess what will happen to the pattern.
See if your guess is correct.

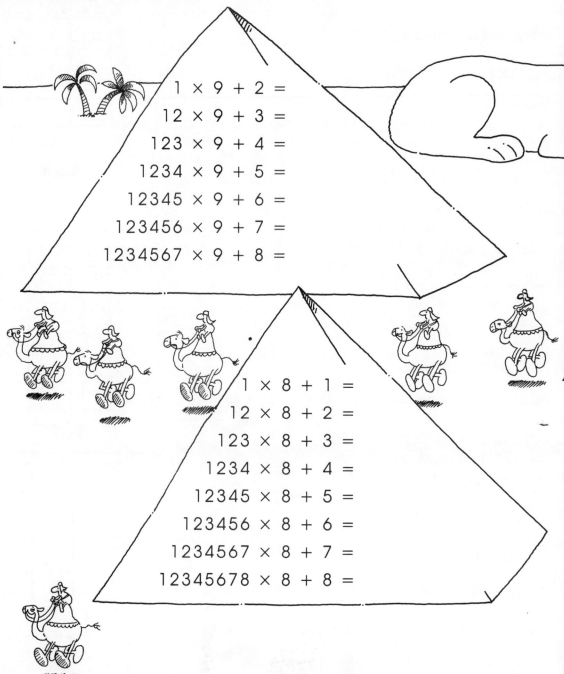

$1 \times 9 + 2 =$

$12 \times 9 + 3 =$

$123 \times 9 + 4 =$

$1234 \times 9 + 5 =$

$12345 \times 9 + 6 =$

$123456 \times 9 + 7 =$

$1234567 \times 9 + 8 =$

$1 \times 8 + 1 =$

$12 \times 8 + 2 =$

$123 \times 8 + 3 =$

$1234 \times 8 + 4 =$

$12345 \times 8 + 5 =$

$123456 \times 8 + 6 =$

$1234567 \times 8 + 7 =$

$12345678 \times 8 + 8 =$

The child should observe the pattern in the first few examples and then predict what the remaining pattern will be before checking with the calculator.

8

7 PYRAMID PATTERNS

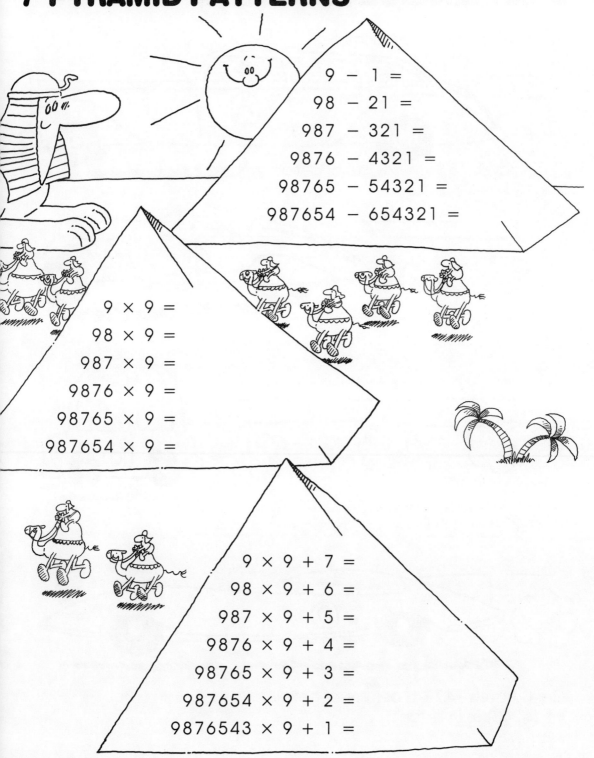

$9 - 1 =$

$98 - 21 =$

$987 - 321 =$

$9876 - 4321 =$

$98765 - 54321 =$

$987654 - 654321 =$

$9 \times 9 =$

$98 \times 9 =$

$987 \times 9 =$

$9876 \times 9 =$

$98765 \times 9 =$

$987654 \times 9 =$

$9 \times 9 + 7 =$

$98 \times 9 + 6 =$

$987 \times 9 + 5 =$

$9876 \times 9 + 4 =$

$98765 \times 9 + 3 =$

$987654 \times 9 + 2 =$

$9876543 \times 9 + 1 =$

8 MAKE A GUESS

Guess which car will go furthest.

Car A travels 13.3 km per litre of petrol.
It has 26 litres in its tank.

Car B travels 15.2 km per litre of petrol.
It has 22 litres in its tank.

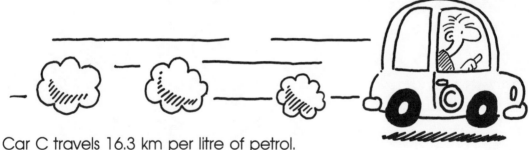

Car C travels 16.3 km per litre of petrol.
It has 21.5 litres in its tank.

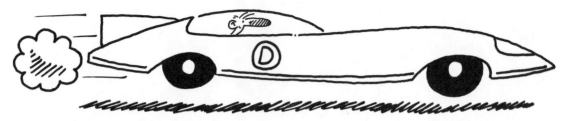

Car D travels 14.7 km per litre of petrol.
It has 24 litres in its tank.

Check if you were correct.

Check that the child understands what 13.3 km per litre means.

9 LIFT OFF

Fill in the missing numbers to launch the spaceship.

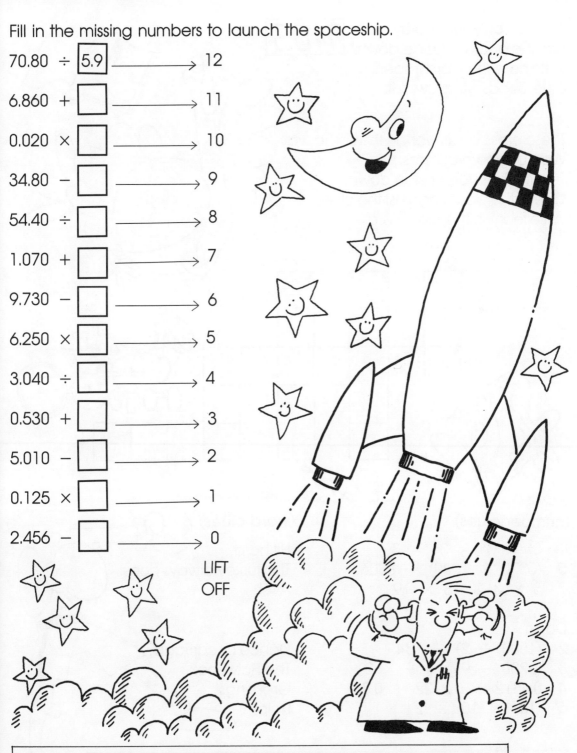

70.80 ÷ [5.9] ⟶ 12

6.860 + [ ] ⟶ 11

0.020 × [ ] ⟶ 10

34.80 − [ ] ⟶ 9

54.40 ÷ [ ] ⟶ 8

1.070 + [ ] ⟶ 7

9.730 − [ ] ⟶ 6

6.250 × [ ] ⟶ 5

3.040 ÷ [ ] ⟶ 4

0.530 + [ ] ⟶ 3

5.010 − [ ] ⟶ 2

0.125 × [ ] ⟶ 1

2.456 − [ ] ⟶ 0

LIFT
OFF

The child may have difficulty trying to fill the boxes by trial and error. It will be easier if she works backwards from the answer.

eg 3.040 ÷ [ ] → 4   3.040 ÷ 4 → [ ]

11

10 NUMBER WORDS ON DISPLAY

Put 7105 on your display.
Turn the display upside down.
Write here the word it spells.
Clue: Seeds will grow in it.

7105

These crosswords work in the same way.
Work out the problems.
Turn the answers upside down.
Check the words against the clues.
Write them in the crossword.

Across
(number clues)

1. $5^2 \times 3^2 \times 3^2 \times 3$
5. $(5370 \times 1000) + 8806$
7. $5 \times 3 \times 13 \times 19$

(word clues)

Hit hard
The turkey always does.
A fish

Down

2. $(1500 \div 2) - 134$
3. $(2200 - 99) \times 9 \times 2$
4. $0.4812 + 0.2122 + 0.08$
6. $(101 \times 10) \div 2$

Dance or carriage?
The Holy Book
Greetings!
Help!

While working at the number clues, make sure the child understands it is necessary to work examples within the brackets first, and understands that 5^2 means 5×5 and 3^2 means 3×3.

11 NUMBER WORDS ON DISPLAY

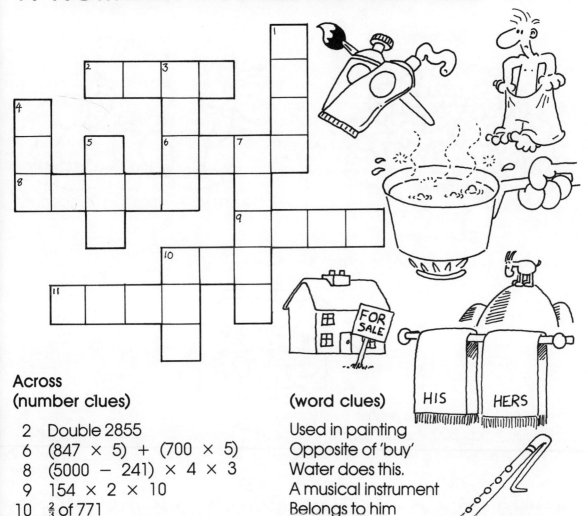

Across

(number clues)

2   Double 2855
6   $(847 \times 5) + (700 \times 5)$
8   $(5000 - 241) \times 4 \times 3$
9   $154 \times 2 \times 10$
10 $\frac{2}{3}$ of 771
11 $\frac{705}{1000}$

(word clues)

Used in painting
Opposite of 'buy'
Water does this.
A musical instrument
Belongs to him
On your own

Down

1   $2204 \div 2 \times 7$
3   $(3^2 \times 615) + 2$
4   1616 halved
5   $(99 + 4) \times 6$
7   $(847 + 820) \times 3 \times 7$
10 $1000 - 196$

You can climb this.
Opposite of 'more'
A boy's name
Large
Not tight
Found in an old fireplace

$263697 \times 7 \times 3$ makes:
Clue: It will not stand up!
Can you make a longer word than this?

12 CATERPILLAR FACTS

This tree is 19.04 metres tall.

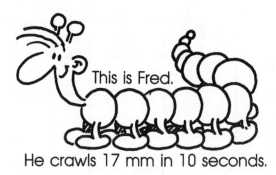

This is Fred.

He crawls 17 mm in 10 seconds.

How long will it take him to climb the tree?

Fred can drink 5 ml of water every hour.
The well holds 500 litres of water.
How many hours would it take him to drink the well dry?

Fred likes cabbages.
He can eat 1 gram of cabbage a day.
There are 36 cabbages in the garden.
Each cabbage has 26 leaves.
Each leaf weighs 15 grams.

How many days would it take him to clear the cabbage patch?

Ensure the child knows certain facts before starting this page.
eg 10 mm = 1 cm   100 cm = 1 metre   1000 ml = 1 litre   1000 grams = 1 kg

13 SQUARE SUBTRACTIONS

You get a SQUARE NUMBER by multiplying two identical numbers together.

Here are some square numbers:

$9 = (3 \times 3)$ $25 = (5 \times 5)$ $121 = (11 \times 11)$

These answers have been made by subtracting square numbers.

The child needs to understand what a square number is before beginning this page -
eg square numbers are: $2 \times 2 = 4, 3 \times 3 = 9$
Example: $5 = 9 - 4$
5 has been made by subtracting two square numbers, 9 and 4.

14 SNAIL'S PACE

Here is Willie McCrawl.

He is the fastest snail in Scotland.
He lives in Aberdeen and is going to visit all his relatives.
They live in Glasgow, Manchester, Birmingham, Newcastle upon Tyne,
London, Plymouth and Southampton.

Look at the map.
Write, in order, the names of the places he visited in his journey from
Aberdeen to Plymouth.

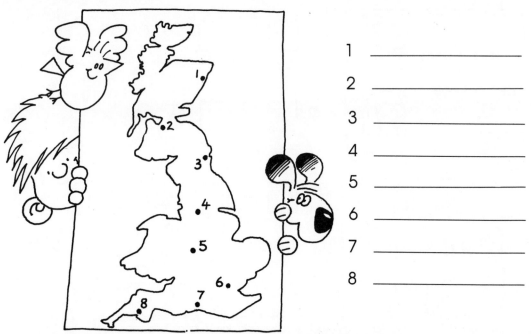

1 _____
2 _____
3 _____
4 _____
5 _____
6 _____
7 _____
8 _____

The child will really need an atlas or road map and may also need help when using the
mileage chart. (eg The distance between Glasgow and Plymouth is 488 miles.)

15 SNAIL'S PACE

Use the chart to find how many miles it is between the places he visited.

London							
492	Aberdeen						
111	411	Birmingham					
389	141	292	Glasgow				
184	333	81	214	Manchester			
274	228	204	145	131	Newcastle upon Tyne		
212	608	206	488	280	407	Plymouth	
77	538	128	419	208	319	148	Southampton

Aberdeen to Glasgow is ☐ miles.

Glasgow to Newcastle upon Tyne is ☐ miles.

Newcastle upon Tyne to Manchester is ☐ miles.

Manchester to Birmingham is ☐ miles.

Birmingham to London is ☐ miles.

London to Southampton is ☐ miles.

Southampton to Plymouth is ☐ miles.

The total distance is ☐ miles.

(1 km = 1000 metres. To change miles to km you ÷ 5, then × 8).

The total distance was ☐ km.

Willie crawled at 50 metres per hour.

It took Willie ☐ hours to crawl 1 km.

The total journey took Willie ☐ hours.

16 DECI-ALIENS LANDING

You can stop the deci-aliens if their total is 1.

Display each number in turn on your calculator.

Input the addition you think will make it 1.

If the display shows 1, then cross out the deci-alien. It is destroyed.

0.6 +	0.8 +
0.3 +	0.5 +
0.7 +	0.2 +
0.4 +	0.94 +
0.61 +	0.16 +
0.33 +	0.47 +
0.82 +	0.66 +
0.11 +	0.59 +
0.25 +	0.79 +
0.76 +	0.99 +
0.78 +	0.42 +
0.38 +	0.74 +
0.81 +	

This activity should help the child with mental addition to 1. Encourage the child to 'count on' from the decimal given. The calculator will provide a check.

0.59 + 0.01 = 0.60

0.60 + 0.4 = 1.00

17 CRACK THE CODE

Find the answer to the coded question.
Here is the key to the code.

A	B	C	D	E	F	G	H	I	J	K	L	M
550	600	650	700	750	800	850	900	950	1000	1050	1100	1150

N	O	P	Q	R	S	T	U	V	W	X	Y	Z
1200	1300	1400	1500	1600	1700	1800	1900	2000	2100	2200	2300	2400

35×60 45×20 50×11 45×40
___   ___   ___   ___

$174 + 776$ $942 + 758$
___   ___

45×40 90×10 30×25
___   ___   ___

$714 + 486$ $257 + 293$ $406 + 744$ $369 + 381$
___   ___   ___   ___

65×20 40×20
___   ___

$257 + 293$ $249 + 551$ $865 + 735$ $174 + 776$ $189 + 461$ $257 + 293$ $888 + 812$
___   ___   ___   ___   ___   ___   ___

$483 + 417$ $174 + 776$ $542 + 308$ $483 + 417$ $369 + 381$ $936 + 764$ $928 + 872$
___   ___   ___   ___   ___   ___   - ___

23×50 65×20 20×95 30×40 45×40 55×10 50×19 30×40 **?**
___   ___   ___   ___   ___   ___   ___   ___

Answer: _____

Accurate use of the calculator is essential to achieve the correct answers. The child should
be encouraged to estimate the answer before using the calculator.
(eg $888 + 812$ - approximately $900 + 800 = 1700$)

18 WHO ARRIVES FIRST?

The snail crawls
20 metres in one day.

Concorde flies
2100 kilometres in one hour.

The snail, train, Alex and Concorde set out at the same time.

The snail crawls for ½ metre.
Concorde flies 1400 kilometres.
The train travels 75 kilometres.
Alex walks 4500 metres.

The first to arrive is _____ .

The last to arrive is _____ .

The train travels
200 kilometres in one hour.

Alex walks
100 metres in one minute.

Check the child knows that 1000 metres = 1 kilometre.

19 HOW RIGHT YOU ARE

Look at these problems.

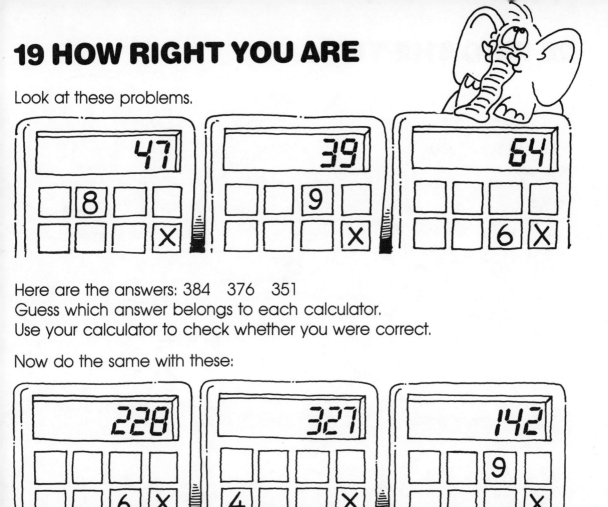

Here are the answers: 384   376   351
Guess which answer belongs to each calculator.
Use your calculator to check whether you were correct.

Now do the same with these:

Here are the answers: 1308   1368   1278

Here are the answers: 1304   1284   1264

It would be helpful if the child found an approximate answer before using the calculator.
(eg 39 × 9 - approximately 40 × 10 = 400)
As a small slip in entering figures could make the answer wrong, the child should be
encouraged to work out an approximate answer before all calculations.

20 FIND THE TWIN

Join the pairs that give the same answer.

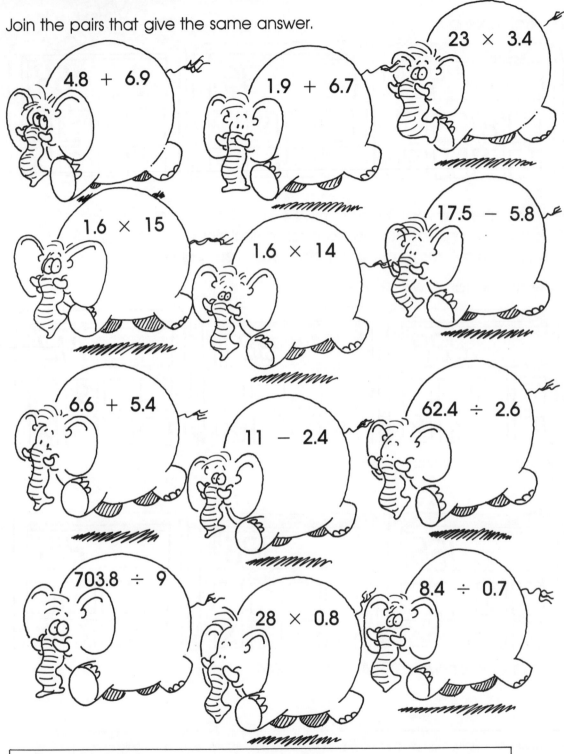

4.8 + 6.9

1.9 + 6.7

23 × 3.4

1.6 × 15

1.6 × 14

17.5 − 5.8

6.6 + 5.4

11 − 2.4

62.4 ÷ 2.6

703.8 ÷ 9

28 × 0.8

8.4 ÷ 0.7

As a misplaced decimal point can provide a wrong answer on the calculator, the child should be encouraged to get an approximate answer first. (eg 703.8 ÷ 9 - approximately 700 ÷ 10 = 70)

21 IT'S MAGIC

Marlo the magician changed:

5642 into 8765 in one step.

His input was + 3123.
Count how many steps you take to change each of these?

START WITH	CHANGE TO	NUMBER OF STEPS
111	121	☐
2222	3456	☐
33333	87654	☐
123123	234567	☐
12345678	23456789	☐

Total number of steps you needed = ☐

If you took less than 15 you can call yourself:

CALCULATOR CHAMPION!

The activity on this page involves work on difference and place value. The child should look
at the difference in each column to arrive at an answer. (eg 4213 to 8646 → units
difference 3, tens difference 3, etc.)

22 TREASURE TRAIL

Which treasure will you find?
Look for the answer to each multiplication in the DIRECTIONS BOX.
This will tell you which direction to move.
Move to the next junction.

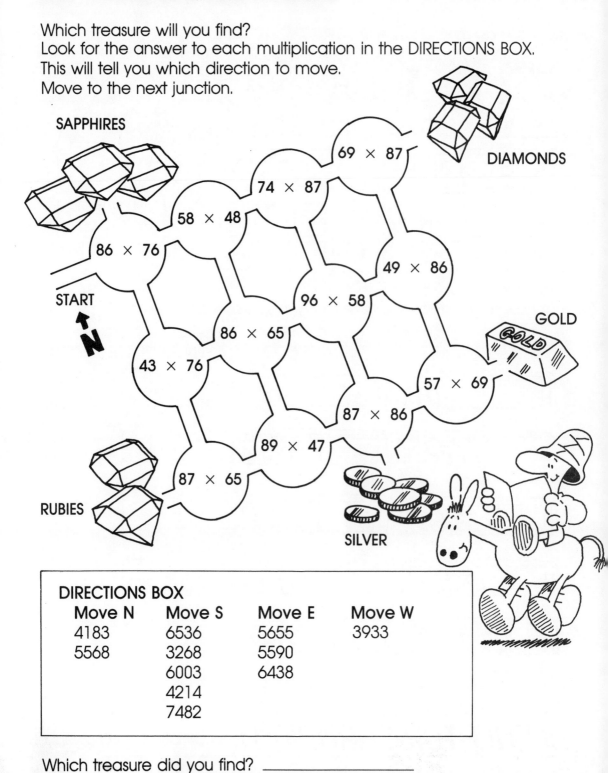

SAPPHIRES

DIAMONDS

69 × 87

74 × 87

58 × 48

86 × 76

49 × 86

START

96 × 58

N

86 × 65

43 × 76

GOLD

57 × 69

87 × 86

89 × 47

RUBIES

87 × 65

SILVER

DIRECTIONS BOX

Move N	Move S	Move E	Move W
4183	6536	5655	3933
5568	3268	5590	
	6003	6438	
	4214		
	7482		

Which treasure did you find? _____

Make sure the child understands N, S, E, W before starting this page.

24

23 NEXT DOOR NUMBERS

240 is made by multiplying two consecutive numbers.

240   Try 1: | 12 × 13 | = | 156 | too small

Try 2: | 16 × 17 | = | 272 | too large

Try 3: | 15 × 16 | = | 240 | just right!

Try to find these consecutive numbers in under four goes:

342   Try 1: [×   ] = [   ]

Try 2: [×   ] = [   ]

Try 3: [×   ] = [   ]

Try 4: [×   ] = [   ]

380   Try 1: [×   ] = [   ]

Try 2: [×   ] = [   ]

Try 3: [×   ] = [   ]

Try 4: [×   ] = [   ]

506   Try 1: [×   ] = [   ]

Try 2: [×   ] = [   ]

Try 3: [×   ] = [   ]

Try 4: [×   ] = [   ]

812   Try 1: [×   ] = [   ]

Try 2: [×   ] = [   ]

Try 3: [×   ] = [   ]

Try 4: [×   ] = [   ]

992   Try 1: [×   ] = [   ]

Try 2: [×   ] = [   ]

Try 3: [×   ] = [   ]

Try 4: [×   ] = [   ]

The child needs to know that consecutive numbers mean numbers next to each other.

24 PATTERNS WITHOUT LIMITS

Put 100 on your display.
Input one division operation to show each of the results below.
Remember to start with 100 on your display each time.

9.090909 100 ÷ ☐ 3.030303 100 ÷ ☐

1.5151515 100 ÷ ☐ 4.5454545 100 ÷ ☐

3.7037037 100 ÷ ☐ 1.2345679 100 ÷ ☐

2.2727272 100 ÷ ☐ 1.8518518 100 ÷ ☐

1.8181818 100 ÷ ☐ 1.010101 100 ÷ ☐

0.9259259 100 ÷ ☐ 0.7575757 100 ÷ ☐

The child should be encouraged to find an approximate answer first so that her attempt is not totally random, (eg 9.090909 – approximately 100 ÷ 10 = 10, so the division must be somewhere near 10.)

25 PATTERNS WITHOUT LIMITS

6.6666666	100 ÷	☐
2.2222222	100 ÷	☐
33.333333	100 ÷	☐
1.1111111	100 ÷	☐
1.3333333	100 ÷	☐
1.6666666	100 ÷	☐
3.3333333	100 ÷	☐
4.1666666	100 ÷	☐
8.3333333	100 ÷	☐
11.111111	100 ÷	☐

26 TIMES AND TIMES AGAIN

These answers have been made by multiplying three consecutive numbers.

24   ☐ × ☐ × ☐

60   ☐ × ☐ × ☐

336   ☐ × ☐ × ☐

504   ☐ × ☐ × ☐

990   ☐ × ☐ × ☐

4080   ☐ × ☐ × ☐

1716   ☐ × ☐ × ☐

6840   ☐ × ☐ × ☐

27 THE BROKEN KEY

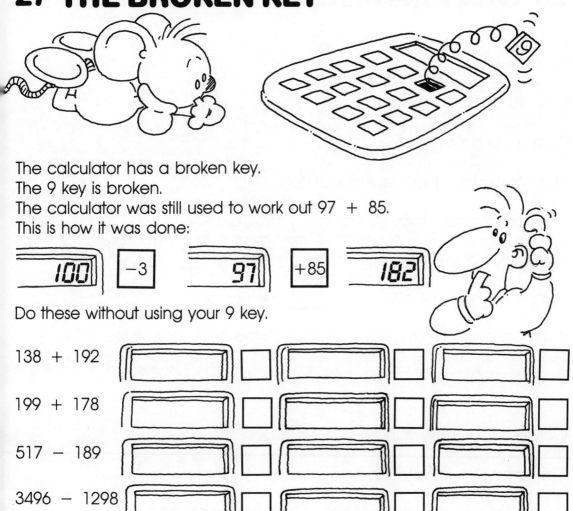

The calculator has a broken key.
The 9 key is broken.
The calculator was still used to work out 97 + 85.
This is how it was done:

| 100 | −3 | 97 | +85 | 182 |

Do these without using your 9 key.

138 + 192

199 + 178

517 − 189

3496 − 1298

75 × 19

189 × 38

711 ÷ 9

8664 ÷ 19

It may be necessary to explain that 9 can appear in the display without pressing the 9 key.
(eg 3 × 3)

28 WHAT AN AGE!

How many minutes have you lived?
Let us use the calculator to find out.

How old are you in years? ☐ years

Change to days (× 365). ☐ days

How many days since your last birthday? ☐ days

Add the days together.	I am ☐ days old.
Multiply the days by 24.	I am ☐ hours old
Multiply the hours by 60.	I am ☐ minutes old.

If you are feeling really clever include all the leap years there have been since you were born.
Now work out how many minutes old you are.

Work out how many minutes you have been at school.

First work out your school day in minutes: ☐ minutes

I have been at school ☐ years ☐ weeks.

× 39 (weeks in a school year)

I have been at school ☐ weeks.

× 5 (days in a school week)

I have been at school ☐ days.

× minutes in your school day

I have been at school ☐ minutes.

Haven't you been at school a long, long time!

ANSWERS

1 Table teaser
When you multiply corner numbers you get the same answer.

2 Conquer the moon
A game, no answers

3 Special keys
There are many ways of getting the answers. Here is one example for each number:
$25 = 9 \times 3 + 4 - 3 - 3$ or $43 + 3 + 4$
$50 = 7 \times 8 - 6$
$50 = 5 \times 8 + 2 + 8$ or 25×2
$100 = 4 \times 4 \times 7 - 8 - 4$
$100 = 3 \times 4 \times 8 + 4$

4 Circular code
I think calculators are tremendous fun.

5 Turn and turn again
You should always get the answer 1089.

6 Pyramid patterns
$1 \times 9 + 2 = 11$
$12 \times 9 + 3 = 111$
$123 \times 9 + 4 = 1111$
$1234 \times 9 + 5 = 11111$
$12345 \times 9 + 6 = 111111$
$123456 \times 9 + 8 = 1111111$
$1234567 \times 9 + 8 = 11111111$

$1 \times 8 + = 9$
$12 \times 8 + 2 = 98$
$123 \times 8 + 3 = 987$
$1234 \times 8 + 4 = 9876$
$12345 \times 8 + 5 = 98765$
$123456 \times 8 + 6 = 987654$
$1234567 \times 8 + 7 = 9876543$
$12345678 \times 8 + 8 = 98765432$

7 Pyramid patterns
$9 - 1 = 8$
$98 - 21 = 77$
$987 - 321 = 666$
$9876 - 4321 = 5555$
$98765 - 54321 = 44444$
$987654 - 654321 = 333333$

$9 \times 9 = 81$
$98 \times 9 = 882$
$987 \times 9 = 8883$
$9876 \times 9 = 88884$
$98765 \times 9 = 888885$
$987654 \times 9 = 8888886$

$9 \times 9 + 7 = 88$
$98 \times 9 + 6 = 888$
$987 \times 9 + 5 = 8888$
$9876 \times 9 + 4 = 88888$
$98765 \times 9 + 3 = 888888$
$987654 \times 9 + 2 = 8888888$
$9876543 \times 9 + 1 = 88888888$

8 Make a guess
A = 345.8 km   B = 334.4 km
C = 350.45 km   D = 352.8 km
D goes the furthest.

9 Lift off
$70.80 \div 5.9$
$6.860 + 4.14$
0.020×500
$34.80 - 25.8$
$54.40 \div 6.8$
$1.070 + 5.93$
$9.730 - 3.73$
6.250×0.8
$3.040 \div 0.76$
$0.530 + 2.47$
$5.010 - 3.01$
0.125×8
$2.456 - 2.456$

10 Number words on display

Across	Down
1 SLOG	2 GIG
5 GOBBLES	3 BIBLE
7 SOLE	4 HELLO
	6 SOS

11 Number words on display

Across	Down
2 OILS	1 HILL
6 SELL	3 LESS
8 BOILS	4 BOB
9 OBOE	5 BIG
10 HIS	7 LOOSE
11 SOLO	10 HOB

12 Caterpillar facts
11200 secs: which is over 3 hours
100,000 hours: which is over 11 years
14040 days: which is over 38 years

13 Square subtractions
There may be other answers to some of these:
$16 = 25 - 9$
$33 = 49 - 16$
$51 = 100 - 49$
$63 = 64 - 1$
$57 = 121 - 64$
$105 = 121 - 16$

14 Snail's pace
1 Aberdeen
2 Glasgow
3 Newcastle upon Tyne
4 Manchester
5 Birmingham
6 London
7 Southampton
8 Plymouth

15 Snail's pace
Aberdeen to Glasgow is 141 miles.
Glasgow to Newcastle upon Tyne is 145 miles.
Newcastle upon Tyne to Manchester is 131 miles.
Manchester to Birmingham is 81 miles.
Birmingham to London is 111 miles.
London to Southampton is 77 miles.
Southampton to Plymouth is 148 miles.

The total distance is 834 miles.

The total distance was 1334.4 km.

The total journey took Willie 26688 hours (about 3 years!).

16 Deci-aliens landing
0.6 + 0.4   0.8 + 0.2   0.3 + 0.7   0.5 + 0.5
0.7 + 0.3   0.2 + 0.8   0.4 + 0.6
0.94 + 0.06   0.61 + 0.39   0.16 + 0.84   0.33 + 0.67
0.47 + 0.53   0.82 + 0.18   0.66 + 0.34
0.79 + 0.21   0.11 + 0.89   0.59 + 0.41   0.25 + 0.75
0.76 + 0.24   0.99 + 0.01   0.78 + 0.22
0.42 + 0.58   0.38 + 0.62   0.74 + 0.26   0.81 + 0.19

17 Crack the code
What is the name of Africa's highest mountain?
The answer is Kilimanjaro.

18 Who arrives first?
The order of arriving is:
1 train   2 snail   3 Concorde   4 Alex

19 How right you are
$47 \times 8 = 376$ $39 \times 9 = 351$
$64 \times 6 = 384$
$228 \times 6 = 1368$ $327 \times 4 = 1308$
$142 \times 9 = 1278$
$158 \times 8 = 1264$ $326 \times 4 = 1304$
$214 \times 6 = 1284$

20 Find the twin
$4.8 + 6.9 = 11.7$ $1.9 + 6.7 = 8.6$
$17.5 - 5.8 = 11.7$ $11 - 2.4 = 8.6$

$1.6 \times 15 = 24$ $23 \times 3.4 = 78.2$
$62.4 \div 2.6 = 24$ $703.8 \div 9 = 78.2$

$1.6 \times 14 = 22.4$ $6.6 + 5.4 = 12$
$28 \times 0.8 = 22.4$ $8.4 \div 0.7 = 12$

21 It's magic
No answers.

22 Treasure trail
You should find the treasure: SILVER

23 Next door numbers
$342 = 18 \times 19$
$380 = 19 \times 20$
$506 = 22 \times 23$
$812 = 28 \times 29$
$992 = 31 \times 32$

24 Patterns without limit
$100 \div 11$ $100 \div 33$
$100 \div 66$ $100 \div 22$
$100 \div 27$ $100 \div 81$
$100 \div 44$ $100 \div 54$
$100 \div 55$ $100 \div 99$
$100 \div 108$ $100 \div 132$

25 Patterns without limit
$100 \div 15$ $100 \div 45$
$100 \div 3$ $100 \div 90$
$100 \div 75$ $100 \div 60$
$100 \div 30$ $100 \div 24$
$100 \div 12$ $100 \div 9$

26 Times and times again
$24 = 2 \times 3 \times 4$
$60 = 3 \times 4 \times 5$
$336 = 6 \times 7 \times 8$
$504 = 7 \times 8 \times 9$
$990 = 9 \times 10 \times 11$
$4080 = 15 \times 16 \times 17$
$1716 = 11 \times 12 \times 13$
$6840 = 18 \times 19 \times 20$

27 The broken key
There are several ways of getting the answers without using the 9 key.
Here is one example of each:
$138 + 192 = 138 + 202 - 10 = 330$
$199 + 178 = 200 + 177 = 377$
$517 - 189 = 517 - 188 - 1 = 328$
$3496 - 1298 = 3500 - 4 - 1300 + 2 = 2198$
$75 \times 19 = 75 \times 20 - 75 = 1425$
$189 \times 38 = 188 \times 38 + 38 = 7182$
$711 \div 9 = 711 \div 18 \times 2 = 79$
$8664 \div 19 = 8664 \div 38 \times 2 = 456$

28 What an age!
No answers.